REAL ALE
Recipes, History & Snippets

1 3 5 7 9 10 8 6 4 2

Published in 2008 by Ebury Press, an imprint of Ebury Publishing

A Random House Group Company

Text written by Bill Laws © Ebury Press 2008

The Random House Group Limited Reg. No. 954009

Addresses for companies within the Random House Group can be found at www.randomhouse.co.uk

A CIP catalogue record for this book is available from the British Library

The Random House Group Limited supports The Forest Stewardship Council (FSC), the leading international forest certification organization. All our titles that are printed on Greenpeace approved FSC certified paper carry the FSC logo. Our paper procurement policy can be found at www.rbooks.co.uk/environment

To buy books by your favourite authors and register for offers visit www.rbooks.co.uk

Printed and bound in Slovenia by MKT PRINT d.d.

ISBN 9780091930219

REAL ALE

Recipes, History & Snippets

BILL LAWS

EBURY
PRESS

Contents

CHAPTER ONE

Beer and Good Ale

At all feasts where ale was strongest
Sat the merry monarch longest,
First to come and last to go.

Henry Longfellow, 'THE MUSICIAN'S TALE', 1867

Let the Brewing Begin

In 2008, Suffolk Gypsy Gordon Boswell commissioned a beer – Romany Bitter – to celebrate his people and their culture. Five thousand years earlier, somewhere in the Middle East, a Sumerian, working with fermented liquid taken from cakes of coarse-ground flour and sweetened with dates and honey, brewed up his first celebratory *kash* ale. Clearly, we have been celebrating real ale for a long time.

In what is now modern Iraq and Syria, the farmers learned to cut their crops and brew their beer – brewing and farming were always close sisters. However, although their scribes were the first to record the brewer's craft for posterity, these were not the world's first brewers. From Africa to Argentina, from Mexico to Murmansk, people have brewed and supped ceremonial ales to mark special events: births, wakes, summer solstices and harvests home.

Basic ale or beer (beer, from the Latin *bibere*, to drink) brought water, processed grain and wild yeasts together into beery beverages that ranged from the poet John Milton's favourite 'spicy nut-brown ale' to Thomas Hardy's fictional Dorchester ale: 'full in body yet brisk as a volcano; piquant, yet without a twang'. It really does take a poet to describe a good ale.

In the 1920s archaeologists in Egypt found a 4,500-year-old figure of a woman. Any Eastern European ale aficionado would have recognized what she was doing: kneading liquid from bread, placed in a basket over a clay vessel. The liquor would have flowed into the vessel where, over the next two or three days, it would brew up into a silky, brown beer. The farmhouse brewers of Russia still enjoy a tipple of their bread beer, kvass.

The civilizing Sumerians who farmed the fertile land between the Tigris and Euphrates before the Egyptians, poshed up the process, eventually using malted grains (sprouted and sun-dried emmer wheat and barley) to create the champagne of Sumerian life.

Although our Egyptian figurine clearly preferred her traditional bread beer recipe, the Babylonians and Egyptians followed suit with their malted ales, even building industrial-style breweries under the blessing of Hathor, the deity who they believed took a benevolent interest in their labours.

Then came the rise of the Mediterranean civilizations whose writers noted how 'the Egyptians drink a wine which they get from barley' (that was Herodotus) while the tribes of Western

Europe created 'an intoxicating drink from corn steeped in water', as Pliny the Elder observed. When his fellow Romans invaded these territories, they brought their own brews and brewers, thank you very much, with them.

Ale, however, had long been a staple part of the British diet when the Romans beached their boats on *terra Britannia*. Vindolanda in Northumberland was one of the most remote reaches of the Roman Empire. As they sought to quell the troublesome Picts, beer played its part in boosting morale. Spidery Roman writing, preserved on slivers of wood in the dried-up silt of the garrison's foundations, reveal that Atrectus the brewer sold the barracks twelve gallons of *cervisia*, and *bracis* (emmer wheat or malt) for the garrison's own brew.

When the Romans departed, northern tribes from the Angles to the Vikings (their Valhalla reputedly revolved around the serious consumption of good ale) moved in, bringing with them their own special brews. It was the Anglo-Saxons' *ealu* – originally the malted alcoholic brew seasoned and preserved with herbs and spices – which gave us our ale.

It is still celebrated in the word 'bridal', or 'bride ale', the special brew of the wedding feast, and the traditional church ale, the sale of which once funded a new roof or a fresh peal of bells for the parish church.

TALES FROM THE TAP ROOM:
SINGING WITH JOY

The Epic of Gilgamesh, inscribed on tablets around 4,000 years ago, describes Enkidu's first taste of ale:

'Shamhat . . . brought him to the hut of the shepherds. They placed food in front of him. They placed beer in front of him. Enkidu knew nothing about eating bread for food: and of drinking beer he had not been taught. The harlot spoke to Enkidu, saying:

"Eat the food, Enkidu, it is the way one lives. Drink the beer, as is the custom of the land."

Enkidu ate the food until he was sated. He drank the beer – seven jugs – and became expansive and sang with joy. He was elated and his face glowed. He splashed his shaggy body with water, and rubbed himself with oil. And turned into a human.'

Beer Bread

Makes 1 loaf

225 G/8 OZ STRONG WHOLEMEAL FLOUR
45 G/1 ½ OZ BUTTER
1 TSP SALT
1 TSP SUGAR
225 G/8 OZ CHEDDAR, COARSELY GRATED
1 SACHET (6 G/¼ OZ) DRIED YEAST
150 ML/¼ PINT ALE, WARMED

Rub butter into flour. Add all the other ingredients and make a dough with the beer. Knead for 10 minutes. Place dough on a greased baking sheet and leave in a warm place to prove until doubled in size. Bake at 180°C/350°F/Gas Mark 4 for approximately 40 minutes until risen and golden.

BEER OR ALE?

Once upon a time beer had added hops, ale had none. Today the words are interchangeable.

Ales Ancient and Modern

In the emerging Middle Ages religious orders provided everything from hospitals to medieval flop houses. While the ale wife catered for the domestic market, busily brewing thin ales for the master's table, the multinational monasteries concentrated on reorganizing the brewing industry. Recipes for best, second-best and visitor-only brews (*prima melior*; *secunda*; *tertia*) were mastered and noted down on parchment; ale barrels were inscribed with the appropriate number of crosses to denote strength and quality (could this be the origins of the Triple XXX?); and the monks settled in the parlour (from the French *parler*, to talk), the forerunner of the lounge bar, to debate the merits of their fellow brothers' latest brew.

It was just as well. The link between latrines and well water was still misunderstood and beer, where the water was boiled, was a safer drink than water.

By the twelfth century the monks, or a brewer they knew very well, had instigated the Great Hop Breakthrough. Hops preserve beer (they flavour it too) and around 1150 the Rhine maiden Abbess Hildegard of Bingen noted that if hops were not to be employed in the brew, the brewer should add a pile of ash leaves.

However, even 'hopping' the ale did not prevent that perennial problem of 'off' beer. When fermentation fell away, especially

in summer, a barrel of sweet, nutty ale could suddenly sour into a brew barely fit for pig swill. It was the Bavarian brethren who accidentally stumbled on a solution when they tried chilling their ale in cool cellars. The yeasts carried on bubbling away, but instead of frothing merrily on top of the brew, they sank to the bottom and bubbled from below. Rather than endure ale-room jests about 'bottom-brewing' beer, the monks christened their baby *Lagerbier* (from the German for storehouse, *Lager*). Josef Groll, no doubt, offered them a prayer of thanks when, in October 1842, he mashed his first perfect, pale *Lagerbier* at the citizens' brewery in Pilsen, Bohemia. One hundred and fifty years later Mr Groll's Pils was the world's leading beer.

In 1882 the Wrexham Lager Beer

Company was the first in Britain to start brewing lager beer. Then, in 1935 another Welsh brewer, at Felinfoel in Llanelli, became the first in Europe to can beer. The history of the can of lager might have been very different if these two brewers had joined forces.

TALES FROM THE TAP ROOM: PRAYER AND ALE

Benedict, the sixth-century father of the Benedictines, and advocate of the spiritual movement *vita apostolica*, advocated obedience, silence, poverty, humility, prayer and beer. It led to the foundation of a Christian empire, the Cistercians (from Cîteaux in Burgundy), who fanned out across northern Europe – Wales alone boasted at least fifteen monasteries – bringing with them their beery wisdom.

The breakaway Trappists, from the Normandy Abbey of La Trappe, founded in 1140, refined the special brew into a top-fermenting, bottle-conditioned ale. The French Revolution and then the First World War put a temporary end to their efforts, but by the 1930s the Trappists were back brewing. When unscrupulous secular brewers tried passing off their own ale as 'Trappist' beers, the monks successfully sued.

Stilton and Stout Pâté

Serves 6

50 G / 2 OZ BUTTER

1 SHALLOT, FINELY CHOPPED

1 GARLIC CLOVE, MINCED

55 ML / 2 FL OZ STOUT

ZEST OF 1 LEMON

110 G / 4 OZ STILTON, CRUMBLED

FRESH PARSLEY, FINELY CHOPPED

Melt butter in saucepan, add the shallot and garlic, and cook gently until soft. Remove from heat and allow to cool. When cool, add the stout and stir gently for three minutes. Then add the remaining ingredients and stir well. Process in a blender until smooth. Check the seasoning and divide between individual ramekins. Cool in the fridge for at least 2 hours before serving.

BULL OR BUSH?

Markets (and bull baiting) were often held at country pubs (hence the Bull), where an ivy-clad bush or ale stake – forerunner of the inn sign – would be hung outside the brew house when the local ale was ready.

CHAPTER TWO

Roll Out the Keg

O Beer! O Hodgson, Guinness, Allsopp, Bass!
Names that should be on every infant's tongue.

C. S. Calverley, BEER, 1861

British Beer

'Forty-five years ago there was not a labourer's family in the parish that did not brew their own beer and enjoy it by their own fireside,' declared that champion of self-sufficiency, William Cobbett, in 1832.

In his day there were three sources of good ale: the home brewer, the pub brewer and the common brewer. The home brew house could provide for the gentleman's manor house or the labourer's cottage. The pub brewer might serve his own and a few neighbouring inns, while the common brewer, who brewed his ale and trucked it around on the dray, dominated the big metropolitan market of London. With the brewers' barley basket, Sussex, Kent, Essex, Suffolk and Norfolk, on his doorstep, and a succession of technical advances such as attemperators, mechanical mashers and Anders Celsius' new thermometer, the common brewer began making serious money.

In 1785 Mr Whitbread fired twenty-four working horses (can you sack a horse?) at his Chiswell Street brewery in London, replacing them with a steam engine, and men like William Younger, Arthur Guinness, William Bass, Samuel Allsopp and George Hodgson rose to the fore. Their beer was strong and cheap, and the Victorians poured it down their throats as fast as they could (they peaked in the 1870s at 265 pints per head a year).

ROLL OUT THE BARREL

When a beer vat collapsed at Henry Meux's brewery in 1814 near Tottenham Court Road in London it released such a flood of ale that it swept eight people to their deaths.

The social reformer Joseph Rowntree protested in 1901 that 'family expenditure of the working classes upon intoxicants cannot be taken at less than six shillings per week, or about one-sixth of the family income'. *Cassell's Magazine*'s London correspondent was equally outraged: 'A poor man to whom every penny is an object, is almost driven when thirsty to take to beer – too often, unfortunately, the beer in question being so adulterated that it helps in the end to increase rather than alleviate his thirst,' he thundered.

Elsewhere in the country, however, beer was – for the most part – a safe and steady drink, softer than farm cider, safer than pump water. In the Midlands, the West Country, Wales and the North, the pub and the home brewer coexisted happily enough. But things were changing. In the brewing centres of Dublin, Bristol, Wrexham, Edinburgh and, above all, in once sleepy little Burton on Trent, things were changing fast.

Two World Wars

TALES FROM THE TAP ROOM: GOING FOR A BURTON

Some of the nation's best brewing water lies in subterranean pools under Burton on Trent, which is why, during the mid-nineteenth century, one pot in every four drunk in Britain hailed from famous Burton. The monks of Burton Abbey had begun brewing with the local spring water, but by the time the Trent became navigable, Burton was home to 32 breweries. Everyone was going for a Burton. (Why the expression should have become RAF slang for a crash is obscure. It may have originated with a Burton's advertisement showing a group of people with one man, who had gone for a pint of Burton, missing.)

UNDER DORA

The First World War and the demands of the Temperance Movement, which had campaigned against liquor for almost a century, led to restricted ale sales under the Defence of the Realm Act (DORA). One publican recalled serving thirsty navvies building a munitions factory in the West Midlands. 'Under

DORA we were only open one hour at midday and the men, four deep, would come through the double doors. Their change was ready on the bar, but you couldn't use the beer engines because of the froth: you just filled galvanized baths with beer and kept dipping the mugs in for the men.'

In the sombre post-war years, when victory felt little different from defeat for the survivors of Passchendaele and the Somme, a glass of good ale was small compensation. 'Shoulder the sky, my lad, and drink your ale,' offered A.E. Housman in his *Last Poems* (1922).

By the Second World War a glass of ale was synonymous with leafy lanes, Vera Lynn and Old England. 'What two ideas are more inseparable than beer and Britannia' queried the clergyman Sydney Smith in *The Smith of Smiths* (1934). Winston Churchill was bound to agree and made sure his Front Line was kept served with real ale.

TALES FROM THE TAP ROOM: SHIPPING REAL ALE

When the German steamship *Deutschland* broke the transatlantic crossing record in 1900 it was not for want of beer. Although she carried only 6,000 bottles of mineral water for all 1,300 passengers and 600 crew, the ship's owners thoughtfully packed 1,700 pint bottles and 10,000 quarts of beer.

During the Second World War, several Spitfires were adapted to transport beer barrels slung under their wings, while the Admiralty sent HMS *Menestheus* to Vancouver to be turned into a floating brewery complete with theatre and cinema, but the Davy Jones brewery's first pint (made with desalinated sea water) was pulled in December 1945, too late to serve the Allied troops.

Beer Waffles with Sour Cream and Cinnamon

Serves 4

110 G/4 OZ PLAIN FLOUR, SIFTED

1 TSP SALT

50 G/2 OZ BUTTER, MELTED

250 ML/8 FL OZ BEER

1 EGG

GRATED ZEST OF 1 LEMON

½ TSP LEMON JUICE

¼ TSP VANILLA EXTRACT
¼ TSP SUGAR

- Mix all ingredients in a bowl, beating until smooth. Let the mixture stand for two hours. Spread batter on waffle iron and bake until crisp and brown.

- For the topping, mix together 500 ml / 18 fl oz of sour cream and 110 g / 4 oz of brown sugar. Dust with ground cinnamon and serve.

WOOD OR ALUMINIUM?

Stanley Grundy, a production worker on wartime Hawker Hurricanes, introduced the aluminium cask; the Society for the Preservation of Beers from the Wood has been fighting a rearguard action ever since.

⇥ CHAPTER THREE ⇤

The Bitter Revolution

Arrived at Three Miles Cross. It now calls itself a 'Temperance
Hotel', and we were told that you could have tea and bread and
butter there but nothing else.

So wrote a disappointed W. H. Hudson,
AFOOT IN ENGLAND (1909)

Still Bitter after All These Years

The hiker hunting a glass of real ale in the 1970s felt as frustrated as Hudson.

Brewers had adopted Pasteur's ideas with a vengeance. Beer no longer bubbled quietly away in the cellar. Now it was filtered, pasteurized and slopped into robust metal kegs from which it was forced, chilled down and carbonated up, under pressure. Keg beers were to real ale what white sliced was to the brown loaf. It left the real-ale fraternity crying into their beer.

In 1971 four men, Bill Mellor, Graham Lees, Michael Hardman and Jim Makin, were sitting in Patrick O'Neill's bar on Ireland's Kerry coast grumbling about the lack of a decent, cask-conditioned ale, one that continued to mature in the cask and was still fermenting lightly even as the pint was pulled. To revive their flagging spirits, they launched a campaign to bring back the beer. Real ale.

Twelve months later CAMRA – the Campaign for the Revitalization of Real Ale, later the Campaign for Real Ale – held their first annual meeting at the Rose Inn, Nuneaton, with assets of 60 pence. Twelve years later CAMRA was buying pubs, engaging in David-and-Goliath battles with big brewers, and spreading the message that it was time for a real ale revival.

The Bitter Revolution began quietly, but moved swiftly. Even as the Ram Brewery in Wandsworth, London, brewing on the same site since 1581, moved out after yet another merger, small breweries boomed to meet the demand for something akin to Hardy's ideal ale with 'the most beautiful colour that the eye of an artist in beer could desire'. (Eldridge Pope of Dorset did the honours with the first Thomas Hardy ale, a brew that matured for up to 25 years.)

In 1972 Martin Sykes restarted his grandfather's pub brewery at Selby. When composer Mike Oldfield finished *Hergest Ridge* he relaxed over a pint of Jones's First Brew, named after *Monty Python*'s Terry Jones and made by Oldfield's flying instructor, Martin Griffiths, at the nearby Penrhos Brewery. Dr Keith Thomas managed to brew up Flag Porter, fermented with yeasts found in a bottle of porter from a shipwreck. The Blue Anchor in Helston, Cornwall, which had been brewing for 600 years, created the punning Prince of Ales for the wedding of Charles and Diana. Andrew Neame from the 425-year-old Shepherd Neame brewery in Kent, brewers of the Bishop's Finger, set up Britain's highest brewery, Tomintoul, in the Highlands. CAMRA's *Real Ale Guide* listed 90 microbreweries in 1977. Within 30 years they were listing over 600.

It's All about Branding

Branding beer is a serious business. Oyster Stout from the Porter House brewpub in Ireland was an obvious choice with its added shellfish, while Skull Splitter, brewed by Britain's most northerly brewery on Orkney, spoke for itself. Welsh ales sounded positively poetic with the lilting Ysbrid y Ddraig (Spirit of the Dragon), Golden Bannua (Golden Nut), Honddu Gold and Pen y Fan.

Essex had Willie Warmer, South Devon Indiana's Bones and Old Speckled Hen (named after an MG car, not a chicken); there was Blandford Forum Badger, Whitby Wallop and Honiton Otter, while Thirsk's Nightmare Porter and the Forest of Dean's Slaughter Porter hinted at the need for moderation. North Yorkshire's Brewers Droop echoed the warning that 'a pint of beer would do him good/a quart would make him lazy'.

Traditional real ales demanded traditional brewing methods: Black Sheep's Riggwelter (a reference to the sheep that cannot rise after falling on its back) was fermented in traditional 'Yorkshire square' fermenting vessels, while Owd Roger was brewed on the old Burton Union system where excess yeasts flowed out into a trough and excess beer flowed back.

TALES FROM THE TAP ROOM: SAMPLING THE PERFECT PINT

- **Choose a local ale (real ale does not always travel well) and watch it being poured gently. (Bottled ales should slide into the glass to keep back the natural sediments.)**

- **Hold up your glass and check for clarity, colour and a reasonable head. (Bubbles beavering up the side of the glass? The glass needs cleaning.)**

- **Sniff. An aroma of hops? A hint of raspberries? Fine.**

29

A trace of cat's bottom and boot polish? It's off, or the pub's beer pipes need a wash out. The sweet smell of mown hay on a midsummer's eve? You've had one too many.

- Taste and swirl: don't swallow yet. Unlike wine tasters, beer tasters drink the good stuff down, nibbling dry crackers and sipping water between samples.

- A hint of honey or Horlicks? A suggestion of caramel or hazelnuts and hops? It's the back of the tongue that senses bitterness, so swallow. And contemplate.

- Pint of the same?

Welsh Rarebit

225 G/8 OZ GRATED CHEDDAR

25G/1 OZ BUTTER

125 ML/4 FL OZ BROWN ALE

1 TSP DRY MUSTARD

½ TSP PAPRIKA

2 EGG YOLKS

- Melt cheese and butter gently in a heavy-based saucepan. Stir in the ale. Sprinkle in mustard and paprika. Stir in egg yolks and warm through. Pour over slices of hot, dry toast. Brown under a hot grill before serving.

MEN OR WOMEN?

Women with their superior taste memories often make better beer tasters than men; in fact, a quarter of CAMRA members are women. In a survey of women drinkers 37 per cent said they would try a real ale . . . if it was served in a stylish glass!

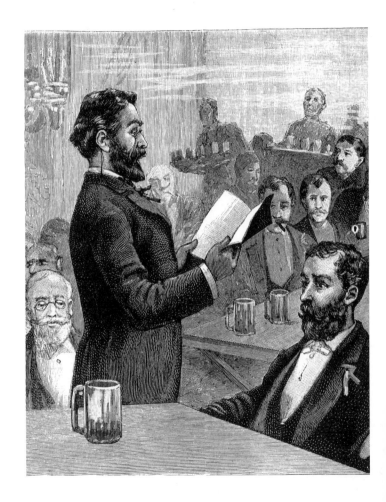

CHAPTER FOUR

First Orders

Dost thou think, because thou art virtuous, there shall be no
more cakes and ale?

William Shakespeare, TWELFTH NIGHT, 1601

Make mine a pint of …

You enter the darkened portal of the Black Swan or Dirty Duck to be confronted by hand pumps (air-pressure pumps in Scotland) and a blackboard listing the brews. Which to choose?

Avoid bland keg beers and start with a local brew with a low alcohol volume of 3.5 or 4 per cent.

BITTER OR MILD?

Originally made to be tippled fresh from the brewery, mild tipped porter into touch at the turn of twentieth century. After the Second World War lightly hopped and malty mild was itself usurped by the drier, hoppier bitters, with their Best or Special versions. Mild, however, remains a favourite pint in the former industrialized parts of Britain. Ask for mild in medieval Wales and you would have received a cloudy pint of unhopped, fresh brew, or *curmi*. Welsh beer is still *cwrwf* and Martyn Cornell, in his *Beer: The Story of the Pint*, suggests this as the root word for the Latin *cervisia* or Spanish *cerveza*.

PINT OF PORTER, LANDLORD

In nineteenth-century London the landlord would pull a pint of dark, strong ale and tell you about how it was named after the capital's strong-arm brigade, the porters who fell for its heavy charms. This was the nation's first industrialized brew, heavily hopped to keep longer, and blended with younger beers for taste. Also dubbed 'entire', it lost out to the lighter ales, although Dublin's Guinness men developed porter into the inimitable pint of dark with (depending on the barman's skills) a shamrock set in the froth.

Is it true that a 'pint of the dark' tastes better in Ireland than anywhere else? Those in the know will explain that the best Irish porter is the one served as a cask-conditioned ale, not a filtered, pasteurized keg beer.

MINE'S A HALF OF STOUT

Samuel Johnson described 'stout' as slang for 'strong beer', but canny brewers advocated its (dubious) medicinal properties, recommending it to 'invalids and nursing mothers'. They even marketed a Nursing Stout as a sensible supplement to mother's milk.

TALES FROM THE TAP ROOM: INDIA PALE ALE

Originally an October ale brewed at London's Bow brewery, India Pale Ale (IPA) would keep for two years in barrel and bottle. Neither from India, nor especially pale, IPA was shipped out to the posh ladies and gentlemen who worked for the East India Company (posh meaning 'portside out, starboard home', the shaded side of the ship on each journey.) The business of brewing IPA was taken over by the Burton's brewers in the early 1800s. It was said (by the Bass brewers of Burton) that the Brits acquired a taste for IPA when a ship carrying barrels of it foundered at sea and the cargo was sold as salvage in Liverpool. A more likely scenario was that the ex-pats demanded more of the same when they returned to the mother country.

DO YOU SELL BRAGGOT?

Not any more. This special brew, a cross between ale and mead, was once the staple beverage in Celtic Britain, a name with echoes in the Welsh for brewer, *bragawd* (and, possibly, in the French *brasseur* and *brasserie*), and which, in the twelfth century, was acceptable as payment of a tithe or tax levied on Welsh serfs.

A DROP OF HEATHER ALE, THEN?

Legend has it that the last-known brewers of the world's most delicious nectar, heather ale, an old father and his son, were imprisoned and told that unless they revealed the mysteries of the brew they would be put to death. The father sidled up to his captors and told them, 'You'll have to kill my son: if he overhears me revealing the secret he will murder me.' The unfortunate lad is led away and dealt with, after which the old man turns to his captors and says: 'Now the poor boy is dead you can slit my throat. For we would never reveal its secrets.'

But someone must have spilt the beans: in 1993 Maclay's Brewery in Alloa began to use native heather tips and myrtle leaves in place of hops for their Heather Ale. (They also brewed a wheat ale with one unusual ingredient: gooseberries.)

A MARMITE SANDWICH AND A VEGGIE ALE, PLEASE?

Something that upsets vegetarians about ale production is the use of isinglass, obtained from fish bladders, and used to clear the ale. Breweries like Black Isle in Ross-shire and Kingstone in Monmouth, however, brew fish-free organic, vegetarian and vegan ales.

A WEE HEAVY?

In Scotland cask ales are still categorized under the ancient 'shilling' system – the weakest at 60/-, the strongest at 90/-. A 'heavy', however, is a heady barley 'wine', which is not a wine, but a super-strong beer.

TALES FROM THE TAP ROOM: BEER AND SKITTLES

Bagatelle and billiards, push-penny and Nine Men's Morris, marbles and quiz nights, phat and Don – there's no end to inventive pub games. Dominoes originated in China and ranks as one of the oldest, while darts (invented by bored militiamen firing arrows at the wooden cask?) goes back at least to Anne Boleyn's time. She presented Henry VIII with a set, but still lost her head. The oddest pub game has to be either West Country Fives, forerunner of the Eton Wall Game (the Anchor Inn near Bridgwater still has its Fives wall) or Ring the Bull, still available at Ye Olde Trip to Jerusalem, Nottingham.

Glazed Leg of Ham with Stout and Cardamom

Serves 4–6 depending on size of ham

1 LEG COOKED HAM

400 ML/14 FL OZ STOUT

110 G/4 OZ BROWN SUGAR

1 TBSP CLEAR HONEY

1 TSP GROUND GINGER

2 TSP DRY MUSTARD

2 TSP GROUND CARDAMOM

- Preheat oven to 170°C/325°F/Gas Mark 3. Remove skin from ham and place in an oven dish, fat side up. Pour the stout over the meat, reserving two tablespoons. Cook in preheated oven for two hours, basting with the stout every so often. Remove from oven and score the fat in a diamond pattern. Mix remaining ingredients with the two tablespoons of stout and spread evenly over the ham. Return to the oven and cook at 200°C/400°F/Gas Mark 6 for 40 minutes.

- Serve with new potatoes, boiled with a sprig of mint.

GOODBODY OR GOING COMMANDO?

When Wye Valley Brewery's Dorothy Goodbody appeared, she was as popular as the contents of her eponymous bottle-conditioned ales. But brewer Peter Amor received a complaint that Dorothy lowered the tone. 'She's just a bit of fun,' insisted the brewer, 'and we're sure she's wearing pants.'

CHAPTER FIVE

Behind Bars

Where village statesmen talked with looks profound
And news much older than their ale went round.

Oliver Goldsmith, THE DESERTED VILLAGE, 1770

Barmaids, Publicans and Pubs

A pub with no beer, an occasion mourned by music-hall singers in the last war, is only marginally worse than a good ale with no pub. Partaking of ale is a sociable business and, besides, the discerning drinker relies on the cellarman to make sure their ale arrives in the glass at its prime.

In Roman times the *publicanus* was a tax collector. No change there then, when you look at the tax on beer (British taxes account for almost a third of the cost of a pint).

Innkeepers, ale keepers and publicans were often colourful characters. Tom Cribb, for example, champion bare-knuckle pugilist at the Napier, High Holborn, and the man he trained, Tom Spring, who ran the neighbouring Castle Tavern, would work out in the bar-room ring, admired by the likes of John Keats and John Clare. Charlie Chaplin's uncle was another London publican, running pubs in Lambeth. He died young: the attrition rate among London publicans was once nine times higher than for other men.

Marie Lloyd, the singer, put her mother to run the Princes Tavern in Wardour Street, London, but if Lloyd George's government had had its way, she would have been out on her ear, since responding to the demands of Temperance campaigners, Lloyd George proposed banning the employment of women in pubs.

But the prospect of driving Britain's barmaids underground was a step too far. After huge demonstrations, the House of Lords threw the Bill out.

In the shires there were less celebrated, but no less renowned landlords, aside from Sid and Jolene pulling pints of Shires at the Bull in Ambridge in BBC Radio's *The Archers*. The innkeeper-cum-gravedigger of the late Cupid's Hill on the Welsh borders at Kentchurch kept the tools of his trade, including his spit-clean, long-handled shovel, propped up in the bar. When pall-bearers stopped at the Cupid's for refreshment – the pub was situated halfway up a steep hill leading to the graveyard – the coffin would be ceremoniously placed on the bagatelle table while a toast was drunk to the recently deceased.

TALES FROM THE TAP ROOM: THE CROWN

It's the commonest pub name in Britain and probably was in the days when the irascible John Taylor, poet and a contemporary of Ben Jonson, ran the Crown in Phoenix Alley, London. During the English Civil War in 1649, when Taylor's beloved King Charles I was beheaded by Oliver Cromwell's Parliamentarians, the landlord renamed his pub the Mourning Crown. Not amused, the Parliamentarians threatened reprisals, prompting the immodest Taylor to rename it the

Poet's Head and setting his own portrait on the inn sign. The publican later tried rowing down the Thames to Queenborough, Kent, in a boat made of brown paper with oars fashioned from two canes and a pair of dead fish. He nearly drowned.

The Last of England

Sometimes it was the pub, not the publican, which rose to the fore. Several London Underground stations owe their name to the pub above them, the Elephant and Castle, Swiss Cottage and the Angel among them. And the Nutshell at Bury St Edmunds could be slipped into the lounge bar of any of them; its internal dimensions, 4.5 m by 2.25 m (roughly 15 by 7 feet), rank it as Britain's smallest pub. Ye Olde Trip to Jerusalem at Nottingham claims to be the oldest in the land, while the Tan Hill Inn, hunkered down in the Yorkshire Dales, is said to be the highest in England. But the inn where most drinkers stare deep in thought at the ceiling is the Pen Y Gwryd in Snowdonia. Everest expedition pioneers, having practised on the North Wales mountains, were in the habit of returning to the Pen and signing their names on the ceiling of the Everest room.

HIKERS' HEAVEN

A pint of real ale and, when the season demands, a roaring log fire in the country inn. Thomas De Quincey, a family friend of Wordsworth, particularly enjoyed such a hostelry south of Dolgellau, Wales, where the mistress of the house worked as cook, waiter, chambermaid, boots and ostler and charged only sixpence for a night's rest.

But in 2003, country inns were closing at the rate of six a week. 'When you have lost your Inns, drown your empty selves, for you will have lost the last of England,' predicted Hilaire Belloc in *This and That* (1925). The prospect of final 'last orders' at Gloucestershire's Beauchamp Arms was too much for the villagers of Dymock (where the clientele once included poets Robert Frost, Rupert Brooke and Edward Thomas). The parish council bought the pub.

TALES FROM THE TAP ROOM: A MAN AND HIS DOG WALKED INTO A PUB

In 1854 farmer George Borrow, having mastered the Welsh language, set off to walk through that country. Reaching Anglesey, which he considered the Isle of Poets, he went in search of a famous bard-publican, but called at the wrong inn. 'Has your master written any poetry?' he asked the serving girl. 'No, sir,' replied the shocked girl. 'My master is a respectable man and would scorn to do anything of that kind.'

Later, he bumped into a man with a dog called Perro. He was curious to know why the man should call it by the Spanish word for 'dog'. 'We call him Perro,' explains the man patiently, 'because he is called Perro.'

Brussels Sprouts in Beer

450 G/1 LB FRESH BRUSSELS SPROUTS
BEER — ENOUGH TO COVER
2 TBSP BUTTER
SEASONING

Trim and wash the sprouts. Place in a medium-sized saucepan and pour in enough beer to cover. Cook for 10 minutes or until tender. Drain and toss in the butter. Season with pepper.

SLEEVER OR HANDLE?

Some swear by the handleless pint glass, or sleever. Others swear at it. While the Belgians prefer their beer in a glass with a stem, the Germans consider the stein cool, not least because it keeps the beer that way. Not cool? Plastic beer cups and pewter tankards dangling from a belt.

CHAPTER SIX

Back to the Brew House

For the hunter he can't hunt the fox nor loudly blow his horn,
And the tinker he can't mend his kettles or his pots without a
bit of barleycorn.

The traditional song, 'JOHN BARLEYCORN'

John Barleycorn in a Nut-brown Bowl

Although brewers, with their liquors, worts (say 'wirts'), mash tuns, floor-malted barleys and cask-conditioned ales, might like you to think otherwise, brewing real ale is not rocket science.

A passable beer can be brewed from maize, millet, rice, palm oil and even – as attempted by a desperate German government in the 1940s – whey. But 5,000 years of brewing suggest that water, sprouted and baked (malted) grain, yeast and a handful of hops are the four essentials.

ADAM'S ALE

'The actual physical condition produced by the free external use of fresh water is in itself a corrective to the craving for liquor.' Setting aside this nineteenth-century exhortation for better bathing, good plain Adam's ale also makes for good ale. And it takes a lot: one litre of beer requires five more of water.

Water in the brewer's bucket becomes liquor from the French *liqueur*, a word that recalls the 'foreign' brewers who crossed the channel in the Middle Ages to help improve English ales. Poor water needs improving or (as they say outside the town with the perfect brewing water, Burton on Trent) 'Burtonizing', that is adding gypsum salts. It's a sensitive business: too much and the ale can act like a laxative.

There are other good brewing waters, for example, at Stratford-upon-Avon, Tadcaster in Yorkshire, Alton in Hampshire and the 'charmed circle' of breweries at Alloa near Stirling (which once boasted nine). However, the suggestion that a great pint of Guinness relied on the waters of the River Liffey in Dublin is unfounded: the liquor was drawn from Dublin's Grand Canal.

Onion Soup with Stout and Watercress

Serves 4

150 ML / ¼ PINT OLIVE OIL

3 LARGE ONIONS, CHOPPED

SEASONING

3½ LITRES (6 PINTS) STOCK

2 SMALL BOTTLES STOUT

1 TSP FRESH THYME

A PINCH ALLSPICE

1 SMALL BUNCH WATERCRESS

- Heat the oil in a large saucepan. Add onions and seasoning and cook with the lid on for 30 minutes. Place all the other ingredients except the watercress into the saucepan and simmer for a further 30 minutes. Season again if required and serve garnished with the watercress.

BARLEY

'Barley, in all the parts and compositions thereof (except malt) is more cooling than wheat, and a little cleansing.'

Culpeper's *Complete Herbal* (1826)

A Suffolk clergyman, the Reverend J. B. Chevallier was passing by a farm labourer's cottage in the 1820s when he spotted an unusual-looking barley growing there. He took the grain seed, grew it on and from it developed a fine variety of brewing barley.

Wheat, oats or rye grain can be 'malted' ready for the brewer, but barley remains a firm favourite among brewers (interestingly even in the 1980s there were Temperance farmers who would no more sell their barley to the brewer than plough their fields on the Sabbath).

According to the traditional song of 'John Barleycorn':

> 'They hired men with the crab trees sticks
> To cut him skin from bone.
> And the miller, he served him worse than that
> For he ground him between two stones.'

First, the maltster must store his grain for a month, then steep it in water (successively soaking and draining it) for two or three days. Then the grain is sprouted, being regularly raked and turned, for five days, when it becomes 'green malt'. This green malt is baked for two days – preferably spread out on the floor of the maltings – before being delivered to the brewers. (The rootlets, or malt culms, are sold on for animal feed – the maltster's barley is like the farm pig: everything but the squeak is used.)

Computer-controlled malting operations now provide the bulk of the malt, but it was not so long ago that it all came down to a practised hand and a good nose. As one seed merchant recalled: 'When farmers brought in their barley samples you didn't analyse it chemically. You just looked at it carefully: "Yup. The malster will like that."'

TALES FROM THE TAP ROOM: BREW UP

A brew begins with mashing, boiling 'hot liquor' and milled, 'malted barley' in the 'mash tun'. The resulting 'mash' is then stood for an hour and a half to allow the starch in the malt to convert into fermentable sugars. The liquid from the mash, the 'wort', is poured into a 'copper', where after the first of the hops have been added, it's boiled vigorously for 90 minutes, after which the second lot of hops is added.

The hopped wort is then chilled before being turned into the fermenting vessels ready for pitching (adding) the yeast. After fermenting for about three days, the beer is chilled then 'racked' into casks where 'isinglass finings' (see also P. 37) are added to allow any yeasts that are left to settle out. The ale now goes through a secondary, slower fermentation in the cask and the brewer has the enviable task of sampling his handiwork before it leaves for the pub.

Jude's Everyday Beer

900 G/2 LBS MALT EXTRACT
900 G/2 LBS SUGAR
50 G/2 OZ FUGGLES HOPS (SEE P.57)
1 STANDARD PACKET BEER YEAST
1 TSP SUGAR AND A DASH OF LEMON JUICE

- You will need two plastic fermenting buckets, a small muslin bag, a thermometer and a plastic beer barrel.

- Start the yeast by placing it in a bottle with the teaspoon of sugar and dash of lemon juice. Shake vigorously and leave in a warm place for a couple of hours.

- Heat 4 gallons of water to around 40ºC, stir in malt extract and sugar and bring to the boil. Add the hops in the muslin bag and boil the wort for 45 minutes. Siphon the wort into the sterilised fermenting bucket, top it up with water to five gallons and, when the wort has cooled to 25ºC, add the yeast.

- Allow ferment to finish (3 to 5 days), siphoning the fermenting wort into the second sterile fermenting bucket after 2 days. Finally transfer the liquid to the beer barrel and allow to mature for 2 to 3 weeks.

The wild service, or chequer, tree (*Sorbus torminalis*) is associated with pubs because its fruit made an ale-like drink. But there is no truth in the tale that the bastard service (*Sorbus x thuringiaca*) earned its name because it was useless for brewing *cervisia*.

CHAPTER SEVEN

Essential Elements

St George he was for England
And before he killed the dragon
He drank a pint of English ale
Out of an English flagon.

G. K. Chesterton, 'THE ENGLISHMAN', 1914

Yeast and Hops

'The vexatious problem of "spoiled beer" seems likely to receive a thoroughly successful solution at last. Pasteur ... has recently given forth his opinion that the chief cause of the "turning" of beer in hot weather, lies in a faulty or abnormal fermentation produced in the process of brewing.

'With pure yeast, and attention to surrounding conditions, Pasteur informs us that a normal fermentation can be induced, and one which remains unchanged by ... the brewer's natural enemy, the sultry heat of summer.' So revealed the 'Gatherer' to readers of *Cassell's Magazine* in the 1890s.

Ale yeasts, *Saccharomyces cervisiae*, are microscopic single-cell organisms which, given the right conditions, convert sugars to alcohol and carbon dioxide gas. Louis Pasteur, who also developed the process of pasteurization, did indeed unravel the mysteries of yeast, revealing it as a complex plant rather than a vague miasma that visited the brewery causing calm – or chaos. The Frenchman used his new-found knowledge to patent a National Revenge Beer (*Bière de la Revanche Nationale*): he was directing his anger at the Germans who had not only dealt France a bloody nose during the Franco-Prussian War, but brewed the better beer.

Pasteur's work was carried on by Copenhagen's Carlsberg

Brewery, where one of the main bottom-brewing yeasts was christened *Saccharomyces carlsbergensis*. Some brewers harvest the excess yeast from one batch of ale to ferment the next, while the Belgian brewers of Lambic beers rely on the random nature of wild yeasts to ferment ales that often have added ingredients such as cherries or raspberries.

And then there was the remarkable discovery, loved or loathed depending on your palate, that a sustaining gluey paste, yeast extract, could be made from the brewer's yeasts. Marmite was born.

Fuggles sounds like a condition induced by oversampling a real ale, but along with Goldings, Pride of Ringwood and Eroica, it is one of the varieties of hops beloved by the brewer. Mr Richard Fuggle of Brenchley, Kent developed his hop at Horsmonden in 1861 and it went on to account for 90 per cent of the hops hurled into the brew. In 1790 Mr Golding's hop of Roughway, Kent, became another of the most widely used.

Although hopped beer was being imported into Britain 600 years ago by the Flemish weavers who had settled in the Kent Wealds, traditionalists held out against beer with added hops for another two centuries. 'I will make it felony to drink small beer,' declared patriotic William Shakespeare in *Henry VI*, referring to the preference for unhopped ales.

But the plant not only gave beer its hoppy flavours, it preserved it for longer.

Soon hop fields ('yards' in Herefordshire and Worcestershire, 'gardens' in Kent) were spreading across the land. The towering hop was grown up strings attached to wires and picked in the hop harvest in late autumn by armies of city families and travelling people, their fingers stained yellow with the natural oils. Picked into a 'crib' and packed into hop pockets, the hop flowers were dried in the oast-houses (kilns in the West Midlands). At its late-nineteenth-century peak there were over 70,000 acres of hops growing in England.

Fish in Beer Batter

Serves 4

175 G / 6 OZ COD, HADDOCK OR OTHER WHITE FISH
CORNFLOUR FOR DUSTING
200 G / 7 OZ PLAIN FLOUR
SEASONING
310 ML / 10½ FL OZ BEER
OIL FOR DEEP FRYING

- Dust fish with cornflour. Season the flour, then add the beer slowly to make a smooth batter. Dip fish in batter and fry in hot oil until brown.

TALES FROM THE TAP ROOM: ADDED EXTRAS

From sugars and spices to bog myrtle (*Myrica gale*) and meadowsweet (*Filipendula ulmaria*) which has similar properties to aspirin, all kinds of things were, and are, added to real ale. Honey was a natural favourite as it sweetened the drink and added natural sugars to aid fermentation, as did fruits such as cherries and raspberries.

Less welcome were additives which benefited the brewer more than the customer. In the nineteenth century, salts were added to increase the volume of ale, but the crime most often levelled at the brewers was of watering down the beer. It was the task of the ale-conners of the Middle Ages to check the quality, and miscreant 'brewsters', or women brewers, could be subject to fines and the ducking stool, where they were strapped to a chair on the end of a pole and ducked in the village pond.

Chocolate Stout Cake with Almonds

Serves 8

110 G / 4 OZ SOFT BUTTER

275 G / 10 OZ BROWN SUGAR

200 ML / 7 FL OZ STOUT

50 G / 2 OZ COCOA POWDER

2 LARGE EGGS

175 G / 6 OZ PLAIN FLOUR

¼ TSP BAKING POWDER

1 TSP BICARBONATE OF SODA

For the icing

    110 G / 4 OZ ICING SUGAR

    50 G / 2 OZ BUTTER

    2 TBSP STOUT

    110 G / 4 OZ DARK CHOCOLATE, MELTED

    50 G / 2 OZ ALMONDS

- Preheat the oven to 180°C/350°F/Gas Mark 4.

- Cream the butter and sugar together until smooth and fluffy. Mix the stout with the cocoa powder. Beat the eggs and add to the butter mixture a little at a time. Fold in the flour, baking powder and bicarbonate of soda, then gradually add the cocoa and stout mixture. Divide cake batter between two 20-cm/8-in sponge tins, greased and lined. Bake in the preheated oven until risen and springy (approximately 30 minutes). Leave to cool before icing.

- To make the icing, beat the icing sugar and butter together. Add the stout and melted chocolate and mix well. Use one third of the icing to sandwich the cake together and spread the remaining mixture over the top. Decorate with almonds.

QUART POT OR BROWN BOWL?

The words of the traditional drinking song list the
publican's measures:

'Here's good luck to the quart pot, good luck to the
Barley Mow
Jolly good luck to the quart pot, good luck to the
Barley Mow,
To the quart pot, half a pint, gill pot, half-a-gill, quarter gill,
nipperkin and a brown bowl,
Here's good luck, good luck to the Barley Mow.'

ACKNOWLEDGEMENTS

Iain Lowe and CAMRA, Peter Amor and the Wye Valley Brewery, Clair Gough for the recipes, Jude Cooper, Sandy Green, Michael Hardman and the Society of Independent Brewers, Davy Petts, Barry Ray, Jerry Ross and Shona Warnes.

FURTHER READING

Borrow, George, WILD WALES (T. Nelson & Sons, 1862)

Bruning, Ted, THE MICROBREWERS' HANDBOOK, Navigator Guides (Melton Constable, 2007).

CASSELL'S MAGAZINE, Cassell (Peter & Galpin, 1890).

Clifford, Sue and King, Angela (editors), ENGLAND IN PARTICULAR (Hodder & Stoughton, 2006).

Cobbett, William, COTTAGE ECONOMY (Verey & Von Kanitz Publishing, 2000).

Cornell, Martyn, BEER: THE STORY OF THE PINT (Headline, 2003).

Culpeper, COMPLETE HERBAL AND ENGLISH PHYSICIAN (Harvey Sales, 1981).

Delderfield, Eric R., INNS AND THEIR SIGNS (David & Charles, 1975).

Girouard, Mark, Victorian Pubs (Yale University Press, 1984).

Glover, Brian, The World Encyclopedia of Beer (Lorenz, 1997).

Harmsworth Magazine, London, 1901.

Hudson, W. H., Afoot in England (J. M. Dent, 1924).

Hurt, Nick and Hurt, Charlie, The Quest for the Perfect Pub (Sidgwick & Jackson, 1989).

Laws, Bill (editor), In The Munitions (Logaston Press, 2003).

Laws, Bill, Byways, Boots & Blisters (The History Press, 2008).

Mabey, Richard, Flora Britannica (Sinclair-Stevenson, 1996).

Protz, Roger and Millns, Tony (editors), Called to the Bar (CAMRA, 1992).

Roud, Steve, The English Year (Penguin, 2006).

Wheeler, Graham and Protz, Roger, Brew Your Own Real Ale at Home (CAMRA, 1993).